D0105196

The World of Children

The World of Children

The Pleasures of Childhood
In Favorite Writings

Selected by William Garvin
Illustrated by Frances Hook

♛

HALLMARK EDITIONS

"A Child's World" from *The Sense of Wonder* by Rachel Carson. Copyright 1956 by Rachel Carson. Reprinted by permission of Harper & Row, Publishers, Inc. "A Memory Full of Charm" from pp. 109-114 in *Mark Twain's Autobiography, Vol I*. Copyright, 1924 by Clara Gabrilowitsch; copyright renewed 1952 by Clara Clemens Samossoud. By permission of Harper & Row, Publishers, Inc. "I Hope You Like Boys" from *Introduction to Modern English and American Literature* by W. Somerset Maugham. Copyright © 1943 by W. Somerset Maugham. Reprinted by permission of the Literary Executor of W. Somerset Maugham. "In Speling I Got 100%" from *Small Voices* by Josef and Dorothy Berger. Copyright © 1966 by Josef and Dorothy Berger. Reprinted by permission of the Publisher, Paul S. Eriksson, Inc. "My Pop Is Tops" from *Write Me a Poem, Baby* by H. Allen Smith. Copyright © 1956, by H. Allen Smith. By permission of Little, Brown and Company. "The Day Time Began" by Eugene McCarthy. Copyright © 1968 by Eugene McCarthy. Reprinted by permission of Eugene McCarthy. "Only in Sleep" from *Collected Poems* of Sara Teasdale by Sara Teasdale. Copyright 1937-1966 by Sara Teasdale and Morgan Guaranty Trust Co. of New York. Reprinted by permission of Morgan Guaranty Trust Company of New York, Trustee. "Laced With Many Golden Threads" from *This Is Eric Sevareid* by Eric Sevareid. Copyright 1964 by Eric Sevareid. Reprinted by permission of Harold Matson Company, Inc. "Little Abe" from *Abraham Lincoln* by Benjamin P. Thomas. Copyright 1952 by Benjamin P. Thomas. Reprinted by permission of Alfred A. Knopf, Inc. "The Young Violinist" Copyright © 1963 by Virginia Sorensen. Reprinted from "The Secret Summer" in *Where Nothing Is Long Ago: Memories of a Mormon Childhood* by permission of Harcourt, Brace & World, Inc. "To Do as You Please" from *Life Among the Giants* by Leontine Young. Copyright © 1966, 1967 by Leontine Young. Used with permission of McGraw-Hill Book Company. "A Girl's First Kiss" from *The Diary of a Young Girl* by Anne Frank. Copyright 1952 by Otto Frank; "The Most Important Day" from *The Story of My Life* by Helen Keller. Copyright 1902, 1903, 1905 by Helen Keller; "Pizza Pies and Fig Bars" from *The Snake Has all the Lines* by Jean Kerr. Copyright © 1958, 1959, 1960 by Jean Kerr; "Sauce for the Gander" from *At Ease: Stories I Tell My Friends* by Dwight David Eisenhower. Copyright © 1967 by Dwight David Eisenhower; all used by permission of Doubleday & Company, Inc. "Love of Ritual" from *The World of Children*. Reproduced by permission of The Hamlyn Publishing Group Limited. "Letters to the President" from *John F. Kennedy and the Young People of America,* Compiled and Edited by Bill Adler, Copyright © 1965 by Bill Adler. Reprinted by permission of the publisher, David McKay Company, Inc. "A Parent's Mission" from *Everything But Money* by Sam Levenson, © 1949-1966 by Sam Levenson; "Table Talk" from *The Parent from Zero to Ten* by Anne Cleveland, Copyright 1957, both reprinted by permission of Simon & Schuster, Inc. "How He Spelt It," "Us Barberryians" and "With Chartroose Flowers" from the book, *Small Voices,* by Josef and Dorothy Berger, © 1966. Reprinted by permission of the Publisher, Paul S. Eriksson, Inc. "A Cow Has Six Sides" and "Girls Are . . . ." from *Write Me a Poem, Baby* by H. Allen Smith, Copyright © 1956, by H. Allen Smith, by permission of Little, Brown and Company: "To Enter the Kingdom of Heaven" from the *Revised Standard Version Bible*. Reprinted by permission of the National Council of the Churches of Christ. "The Idealism of Youth" from *Memoirs of Childhood and Youth* by Albert Schweitzer. Published by Macmillan Company, 1949. Reprinted by permission of the Macmillan Co.

Copyright © 1970 by Hallmark Cards, Inc., Kansas City, Missouri. All Rights Reserved. Printed in the United States of America. Library of Congress Catalog Card Number: 74-102170 Standard Book Number: 87529-062-0.

IN THE WORDS OF
A CHILD

'MY POP IS TOPS'

Personal narratives by children are unique. Their candid freshness and humorous insights provide much pleasure for adults. Here a young boy's entry in a contest for the best essay about fathers wins high honors for delightful description:

We have such good fun with my daddy I wisht I had knew him sooner.

He taked me fishin he taked me hunting, once he even taked me to the burlest show. It was wonderful.

He is a farmer. He smells like a cow and when I smell that cow in the house I know Pop is home and I am glad.

My pop is tops because every time I ast him for a knickel he will start preeching that when he was a boy he had to earn his kenickls and at the same time he is puting his hand in his pocket and pulls out a kinckel, saying this is the last kinkel I have.

My Pop's tops because he was a brave soldier. He didn't see me until I was three years old yet he is just as good to me as if he knew me all my life.

'IN SPELING I GOT 100%'

When Emily Wortis was seven years old her grandfather presented her with a blank book—a diary. Unaided by her parents, Emily showed a flair for honesty, if not spelling:

October 2, 1945. Sadiday. Today I vomited.

Sunday. The first thing I did was, well I heard a cat's voice do you no we have one? by the way lests go on with our diary I climbed down 3 flights of stairs and when I open the door there was a big black cat not ours boy was I mad.

Thursday. Today was assembly in school we saw two plays and slides they were boring. When we came bak our class was being varnished. In the afternoon Joel was supposed to take a seat but said he wud like to set by me what a day

Monday. Today four 5 A girls came in our class and three 8B girls came and two 6 A boys came in. And everyone new me becose I am the president of the class in speling I got 100%.

Saturday, November 5. I played with my pepper-dolls. . . .

January 10, 1946. Wensday. When I came home I rang the bell Daddy ancerd he hid behind the door but I fond him. Goodby. Emily Wortis.

MARS BARS

The Space Age has provided children with a new type of hero . . . and a new ambition. In this brief essay written as a school assignment, an 8-year-old boy, Lee Garvin, tells what he would like to be when he grows up:

Would you like to be an Astronaut? Yes, I would like to see what it is like up in space. I would like to see what it is like on Mars. I could get a lot of candy there. I would like to land on Mercury so I could go swimming in the hot hot weather.

If my father were an astronaut everybody would be talking about him. Everybody would like him too.

'HOW HE SPELT IT'

Here ten-year-old diarist Caroline Cowles Richards describes the highlight of a schoolday in 1852 and displays a touch of sour grapes on the subject of pears:

Today a nice old gentleman by the name of Mr. William Wood visited our school. Wood Street is named after him. He had a beautiful pear in his hand and said he would give it to the boy or girl

who could spell "Virgaloo," for that was the name of the pear. I spelt it but it was not right. A little boy named William Schley spelt it right and he got the pear. I wish I had, but I can't even remember now how he spelt it. If the pear was as hard as its name, I don't believe anyone would want it.

'I HOPE YOU LIKE BOYS'

During World War II, when Britain was under constant attack by German bombers, plans were made to send many children abroad to the safety of America. Hearing of the plan, a ten-year-old English boy wrote this letter of thanks to an American newspaper, the New York Herald-Tribune:

July 1940—I am glad you want us poorer class children as well. I hope to come to America soon not because I'm scared of the bombs or Old Hitler but because I want to see the world and to go on a liner and to see the New York World's Fair. I hope you like boys in America. I should like to live with jolly people near an aerodrome because I'm very keen on aeronautics. I am 10, have just passed my exams and have been awarded a special place at the St. Alban Country School for Boys. I hope

9

I shall be able to go to a Secondary School in America. I have heard your paper quoted by the British Broadcasting Corporation so often so it must be a very reliable paper. I shall probably take it, although my Mother is going to send me the *Overseas Daily Mirror* every week. I thought you would like to know my mother says the working class at any rate will appreciate what you are doing for us.

WITH CHARTROOSE FLOWERS

Although she earned $1,000 a week, ten year-old actress Margaret O'Brien kept a prudent eye on all expenses, as in this case when she bought her mother a hat. This selection from her diary appears in Small Voices, *edited by Josef and Dorothy Berger:*

February 10. A man came out to the set today with four hats. One they are going to use in the picture, but there was another one that was the most beautiful hat I ever saw. I knew it would look perfect on Mama. It was her favorite color too—American Beauty with American Beauty and chartroose velvet flowers on it and a big bow in the back. I asked the man how much it was and he said sixty dollars. Imagine that! —sixty whole dollars for a hat. He said the reason was—it was a Lili Dashay. I told him I wanted to buy it for Mama but I only had $14 and 65 cents in my bank. And he decided to do it, so he gave me the hat and he's coming back tomorrow for his money. I still think even $14 and 65 cents is a lot of money for a hat. Mama was so happy when she saw it she almost cried. She tried it on and she really looks beautiful in it. She said, "It's the most beautiful hat I ever saw." So now I don't care if I spent my money. I didn't have enough to buy a pony anyway, and where would I keep it if I did have one?

'GIRLS ARE . . .'

More than 75 years ago, Mark Twain published an amusing collection of "compositions by students" called English As She is Taught. *The following is a classic expression of a young boy's attitude toward girls:*

Girls are very stuck up and dignefied in their maner and be have your. They think more of dress than anything and like to play with dowls and rags. They cry if they see a cow in a far distance and are afraid of guns. They stay at home all the time and go to church on Sunday. They are al-ways sick. They are al-ways funy and making fun of boy's

hands and they say how dirty. They cant play mar-
bels. I pity them poor things. They make fun of
boys and then turn around and love them. I dont
beleave they every kiled a cat or anything. They
look out every nite and say oh ant the moon lovely.
Thir is one thing I have not told and that is they
always now their lessons bettern boys.

YOUNG POETS LAUREATE

*The following verses and random observations
were written by children in three different
countries—the United States, Canada, and
New Zealand. All the children were eleven
or younger at the time of writing:*

MIRROR! MIRROR!

As I look into the mirror I see my face.
Then I talk to myself.
Then I play like I am in jail.
I pretend that I am bad.
I pretend sometimes that I am on a stage.
I sing to myself. I introduce people.

Deborah Ensign, age 7, U.S.

THE BIRDS ARE SINGING MUSIC

The birds are singing music
because the sun is shining.
I look at the sun with my eyes
and pretty stripes come.

The dew-bubbles on the grass
are tiny balloons,
for spiders to play with.

The grass looks like lots of tiny trees,
only littler.

Desmond Garton, age 8, New Zealand

WIND IN THE TREES

The wind galing
Sounding like breakers rolling
And whales driving through waves
Their tails splashing the foam,
Fountains spouting from their blowholes
Above the glittering sea
That rushes, roaring onto the black rocks.

Robyn, age 7, New Zealand

WHEN SPRING COMES

When spring comes
I feel like a
Daisy just opening up into a new life.
I feel like running twenty miles
And taking off my heavy coat
And putting on a pair of sneakers.
I feel like I started a new life
And everything is better
Than it was before.
I get faster
In running and I can go swimming outdoors.
It feels like the smell of new flowers
And the animals
Coming up from their holes,
The birds coming back from their vacations.
I love spring.

Michael Patrick, age 10, U.S.

THE SCARED CLOUDS

The clouds are stuck and scared to move
For fear the trees might pinch them.

Hannah Hodgins, age 11, U.S.

RAIN

It's watering time
In the gardens of Heaven
As raindrops tumble
On cities and towns.

Richard Drillich, age 9, U.S.

TABLE TALK

*Children don't always choose the most
appetizing topics to discuss at the dinner table.
The following is an authentic tape-recorded
dinner conversation which appears in Anne
Cleveland's Book,* The Parent From Zero to Ten:

First Child: Daddy, how much blood would there
be if you cut a dinosaur's head off?

Male Parent: I've no idea, Mike. Eat your spaghetti and meat balls.

First Child: Timmy said if you cut a dinosaur's
head off, you'd have a whole swimming pool full
of blood. Is that true, Daddy?

Male Parent: I don't know and I'd prefer not to
discuss it at the table.

First Child: Wow! A whole swimming pool full of

blood! What if you fell in?

Male Parent: I said we would not discuss it any further! Eat your dinos—spaghetti!

Second Child: Mummy, do I really have to have Sandra to my party? She smells funny.

First Child: So do you smell funny.

Second Child: I don't.

First Child: You do.

Second Child: I don't!

First Child: You do too.

Second Child: I don't! Mummy, *do* I smell funny?

First Child: Oh boy, look at me eating my dinosaur! All bloody . . . *(murmuring)* Blood . . . blood. . .

Female Parent: *(Enters with milk)* John! You're not *eating!* How can you expect the children . . .

'US BARBERRYIANS'

Maggie Owen, a young Irish girl who lived with a great-aunt in the early years of this century, wrote these passages in her diary about "a new boy in the town." The selection appears in Small Voices, *edited by Josef and Dorothy Berger:*

There is a new boy in the town visiting his uncle. He is an English boy. His name is Edward. He wears golf breeches with tassels to them at the knees, and fancy stockings. He has skinny legs. He was long sick. It may well be twas the sickness made him skinny. His father is a British soldier in India. He is a fine boy but he talks funny. Bess [servant at Castle Rea] says he talks as if he'd a mouthful of buttermilk and she doesn't like him at all. I think him fine. His uncle brought him to call, and Aunt says he has beautiful manners. I am poor mannered. I slopped me tea on me good wool frock and was colded afterwards. Aunt says tis no wonder the British think us barberryians.

This was a long day. Before tea Edward came over with his uncle. We played at jackstraws. I like Edward fine. It may well be that I'll marry him, do his legs fill out. As he gets to the age of proper breeches they'll not show. I expect it may well be we could keep our secrets from each other.

Edward thinks it would be nice to be married to me but says I'll have to go to live in India as he's to be an army officer the like of his father. I am an adventurous child and would like to go off all the time. I would like to come back to visit with a long gowen I'd have to hold up when I got out of the kerrege, and with a fine silk petticoat that would rustle, and a veil. Wouldent I cut a dash just!

I asked Edward would he like to have some children with me and he acted odd.

A GIRL'S FIRST KISS

Although hiding with her family from the Nazis in German-occupied Amsterdam, 14-year-old Anne Frank nevertheless managed to find romance and experience the rapture of a first kiss. This excerpt is from her famous Diary of a Young Girl:

April 16. Sunday morning, just before eleven o'clock.

Remember yesterday's date, for it is a very important day in my life. Surely it is a great day for every girl when she receives her first kiss. . . .

How did I suddenly come by this kiss? Well, I will tell you.

Yesterday evening at eight o'clock I was sitting with Peter on his divan, it wasn't long before his arm went round me. "Let's move up a bit," I said, "then I don't bump my head against the cupboard." He moved up, almost into the corner, I laid my arm under his and across his back, and he just about buried me, because his arm was hanging on my shoulder.

Now we've sat like this on other occasions, but never so close together as yesterday. He held me firmly against him, my left shoulder against his chest; already my heart began to beat faster, but we had not finished yet. He didn't rest until my head was on his shoulder and his against it. When I sat upright again after about five minutes, he soon took my head in his hands and laid it against him once more. Oh, it was so lovely, I couldn't talk much, the joy was too great. He stroked my cheek and arm a bit awkwardly, played with my curls and our heads lay touching most of the time.

How it came about so suddenly, I don't know, but before we went downstairs he kissed me, through my hair, half on my left cheek, half on my ear; I tore downstairs without looking around, and am simply longing for today!

A COW HAS SIX SIDES

According to H. Allen Smith, a ten-year-old boy who was told to write about a bird and a beast came up with the following composition:

The bird I am going to write about is the Owl. The Owl cannot see at all by day and at night is as blind as a bat.

I do not know much about the Owl, so I will go on to the beast which I am going to choose. It is the Cow. The Cow is a mammal. It has six sides— right, left, upper and below. At the back it has a

tail on which hangs a brush. With this it sends the
flies away so that they do not fall into the milk.
The head is for the purpose of growing horns and
so that the mouth can be somewhere. The horns
are to butt with, and the mouth is to moo with.
Under the cow hangs the milk. It is arranged for
milking. When people milk, the milk comes and
there is never an end to the supply. How the cow
does it I have not yet realized, but it makes more
and more. The cow has a fine sense of smell; one
can smell it far away. This is the reason for the
fresh air in the country. The man cow is called an
ox. It is not a mammal. The cow does not eat
much, but what it eats it eats twice, so that it gets
enough. When it is hungry it moos, and when it
says nothing it is because its inside is all full up
with grass.

LETTERS TO THE PRESIDENT

*President John F. Kennedy held a special
attraction for the children and young people of
America. The letters they wrote to him are
often wonderfully expressive of the thoughts and
feelings of childhood:*

Dear Mr. President,
 Everybody calls you JFK. I wish everybody

would call me HBL. That stands for Horace
Bud Lamston. But they don't. They just call me
Bud. How can I get them to call me HBL
like they call you JFK? I am getting tired of
just plain Bud.

Best wishes to JFK, From HBL
Chicago, Illinois

Dear President Kennedy,

How come since you are President of the USA,
you aren't stuck-up or conceited?

My boyfriend, Roger, is president of his class and
you can't even talk to him.

Yours truly, Betsey W.
Linden, New Jersey

Dear President Kennedy,

Could you please call me on the telephone
some day? Nobody ever calls me. Not even the
wrong number.

A pal, David F.
Little Rock, Arkansas

Dear President Kennedy,

Last night I had a dream. And in this dream,
you called me on the telephone and asked me
to fly with you in your airplane *Air Force 1*.

I know it sounds silly to ask but you didn't

22

happen to have the same dream, did you?

A pal, Arthur G.

Columbus, Ohio

Dear President Kennedy,

When did you know you were going to be the Pres of the whole USA? How old were you when you knew?

I am nine and I know already.

A future Pres of the USA, Ronnie F.

Milwaukee, Wisconsin

Dear JFK,

If I have another brother, I hope my parents name him after you.

I have five brothers already and I told my mother my idea but she said five brothers is enough.

Your good pal, Lawrence H.

Westport, Connecticut

Dear Mr. President,

My mother says I have to drink three glasses of milk every day if I want to be President like you some day.

How much milk do you have to drink just to be Vice-President?

Yours, Andrew W.

Erie, Pennsylvania

Dear President Kennedy,

My name is Mark. I am nine. I'll bet you never heard of me but I heard of you.

That is why I am writing this letter. Now we are even. Now you have heard of me.

Best wishes, Mark L.

New York City

Dear President Kennedy,

I love you. I love you. I love you. I don't care if the whole world knows. Only you I love.

Love, Marilyn F.

New York City

P.S. Please don't tell my boyfriend, Andy, I sent this letter.

Dear Mr. President,

I am crazy about you because you never forget the little people. I am one of the little people. I am 4 feet nine.

Harry A.

Chicago, Illinois

Dear Mr. President,

We all think you are a terrific President except for one thing.

Yesterday in the newspapers you said that everybody should drink lots of milk.

Couldn't you say everybody should drink lots of
ice cream sodas and Cokes? Give us a break.

       Your pals, Richard, Jack, Larry, Mike
Gainesville, Georgia

MEMORIES OF
THE GREEN YEARS

ONLY IN SLEEP

Only in sleep I see their faces,
Children I played with when I was a child,
Louise comes back with her brown hair braided,
Annie with ringlets warm and wild.

Only in sleep Time is forgotten—
What may have come to them, who can know?
Yet we played last night as long ago,
And the doll-house stood at the turn of the stair.

The years had not sharpened
their smooth round faces,
I met their eyes and found them mild—
Do they, too, dream of me, I wonder,
And for them am I, too, a child?

Sara Teasdale

HOW I LEARNED TO THINK

In an interview with a New York newspaper,
Abraham Lincoln remembered an incident that
prompted him to "hunt after an idea," a skill
that enabled him to get along on only six months
of formal schooling:

Well, as to education, the newspapers are correct
—I never went to school more than six months in
my life. I say this, that among my earliest recollec-
tions, I remember how, when a mere child, I used to
get irritated when anybody talked to me in a way I
could not understand. I don't think I ever got
angry at anything else in my life. But that always
disturbed my temper and has ever since. I can remember going to my little bedroom, after hearing
the neighbors talk of an evening with my father,
and spending no small part of the night walking up
and down, trying to make out what was the exact
meaning of some of their, to me, dark sayings. I
could not sleep, though I often tried to, when I
got on such a hunt after an idea, until I had caught
it; and when I thought I had put it in language
plain enough, as I thought, for any boy I knew to
comprehend. This was a kind of passion with me,
and it has stuck by me, for I am never easy now,
when I am handling a thought, till I have bounded

it north, and bounded it south, and bounded it east, and bounded it west.

MY DIARY

In The Innocents Abroad, *Mark Twain recalls with wry humor the rules laid down by adults that could lead to a less than successful career:*

[I am reminded] of the journal I opened with the New Year, once, when I was a boy and a confiding and a willing prey to those impossible schemes of reform which well-meaning old maids and grand-mothers set for the feet of unwary youths at that season of the year—setting oversized tasks for them, which, necessarily failing, as infallibly weaken the boy's strength of will, diminish his confidence in himself, and injure his chances of success in life. Please accept of an extract:

"Monday—Got up, washed, went to bed.

"Tuesday—Got up, washed, went to bed.

"Wednesday—Got up, washed, went to bed.

"Thursday—Got up, washed, went to bed.

"Friday—Got up, washed, went to bed.

"Friday fortnight—Got up, washed, went to bed.

"Following month—Got up, washed, went to bed."

I stopped then, discouraged. Startling events appeared to be too rare, in my career, to render a diary necessary. I still reflect with pride, however, that even at that early age I washed when I got up.

'THE MOST IMPORTANT DAY'

In this poignant recollection from her book,
The Story of My Life, Helen Keller writes of
the triumphant day when, as a blind, deaf child,
she first unraveled the mystery of language:

The most important day I remember in all my life is the one on which my teacher, Anne Mansfield Sullivan, came to me. I am filled with wonder when I consider the immeasurable contrast between the two lives which it connects. It was the third of March, 1887, three months before I was seven years old.

On the afternoon of that eventful day, I stood on the porch, dumb, expectant. I guessed vaguely from my mother's signs and from the hurrying to and fro in the house that something unusual was about to happen, so I went to the door and waited on the steps. The afternoon sun penetrated the mass of honeysuckle that covered the porch, and fell on my upturned face. My fingers lingered almost unconsciously on the familiar leaves and blossoms which had just come forth to greet the sweet southern spring. I did not know what the future held of marvel or surprise for me. Anger and bitterness had preyed upon me continually for weeks and a deep languor had succeeded this passionate struggle.

Have you ever been at sea in a dense fog, when it seemed as if a tangible white darkness shut you in, and the great ship, tense and anxious, groped her way toward the shore with plummet and sounding-line, and you waited with beating heart for something to happen? I was like that ship before my education began, only I was without compass or sounding-line, and had no way of knowing how near the harbor was.

"Light? Give me light!" was the wordless cry of my soul, and the light of love shone on me in that very hour.

I felt approaching footsteps. I stretched out my hand as I supposed to my mother. Someone took it, and I was caught up and held close in the arms of her who had come to reveal all things to me, and, more than all things else, to love me. . . .

One day, while I was playing with my new doll, Miss Sullivan put my big rag doll into my lap also, spelled "d-o-l-l" and tried to make me understand that "d-o-l-l" applied to both. Earlier in the day we had a tussle over the words "m-u-g" and "w-a-t-e-r." Miss Sullivan tried to impress it upon me that "m-u-g" is *mug* and that "w-a-t-e-r" is *water,* but I persisted in confounding the two. In despair she had dropped the subject for the time, only to renew it at the first opportunity. I became impatient at her repeated attempts and, seizing the new doll, I dashed it upon the floor. I was keenly delighted when I felt the fragments of the broken doll at my feet. Neither sorrow nor regret followed my passionate outburst. I had not loved the doll. In the still, dark world in which I lived there was no strong sentiment or tenderness. I felt my teacher sweep the fragments to one side of the hearth, and I had a sense of satisfaction that the cause of my discomfort was removed. She brought me my hat, and I knew I was going out into the warm sunshine. This thought, if a wordless sensation may be called a thought, made me hop and skip with pleasure.

We walked down the path to the well-house, attracted by the fragrance of the honeysuckle with which it was covered. Someone was drawing water and my teacher placed my hand under the spout. As the cool stream gushed over one hand she spelled into the other the word *water* first slowly, then rapidly. I stood still, my whole attention fixed upon the motions of her fingers. Suddenly I felt a misty consciousness as of something forgotten—a thrill of

returning thought; and somehow the mystery of a language was revealed to me. I knew then that "w-a-t-e-r" meant the wonderful cool something that was flowing over my hand. That living word awakened my soul, gave it light, hope, joy, set it free! There were barriers still, it is true, but barriers that could in time be swept away.

I left the well-house eager to learn. Everything had a name, and each name gave birth to a new thought. As we returned to the house every object which I touched seemed to quiver with life. That was because I saw everything with the strange, new sight that had come to me. On entering the door I remembered the doll I had broken. I felt my way to the hearth and picked up the pieces. I tried vainly to put them together. Then my eyes filled with tears; for I realized what I had done, and for the first time I felt repentance and sorrow.

I learned a great many new words that day. I do not remember what they all were; but I do know that *mother, father, sister, teacher* were among them—words that were to make the world blossom for me, "like Aaron's rod, with flowers." It would have been difficult to find a happier child than I was as I lay in my crib at the close of that eventful day and lived over the joys it had brought me, and for the first time longed for a new day to come.

SAUCE FOR THE GANDER

In his autobiographical reminiscence, At Ease:
Stories I Tell To Friends, *Dwight Eisenhower
recalls a boyhood incident in which he learned
how "to negotiate with an adversary":*

My earliest memory involves an incident that oc-
curred just before my fifth birthday. My mother's
sister, Aunt Minnie, had been staying with us in
Abilene—we lived in a cottage on Second Street
then—and she took me back with her to Topeka
for a visit. There was the train, and then a long
horse-and-buggy ride to my relatives' farm. I remember looking down through the floorboards,
watching the ground rush past under the horses'
feet.

When we arrived, it seemed that there were
dozens of grown-ups in the house. Even though they
were, somehow, my family, I felt lonesome and lost
among them and I began to wander around outside.

In the rear of the house was a pair of barnyard
geese. The male had no intention of permitting me
to penetrate his domain. Each time he saw me he
would push along toward me with such a hideous
hissing that my five-year-old courage couldn't stand
the strain. I would race for the house, burst into

the kitchen and tell any available elder about this awful old gander.

After several such skirmishes, Uncle Luther decided that something had to be done. He took an old broom and cut off all the straw, leaving a short, hard knob. He showed me how to swing the weapon, then took me out and announced that I was on my own. More frightened at the moment of my uncle's possible scolding than of the gander's aggression, I took what was meant to be a firm, but was really a trembling stand next time the fowl came close. Then I let out a yell and rushed toward him, swinging the club. He turned and I gave him a satisfying smack right on the fanny. He let out a squawk and ran off. From then on I was the proud boss of the backyard. I had learned never to negotiate with an adversary except from a position of strength.

. . . New adams, unhurried, pure, we checked
                         the names
given by the old.
Some things we found well titled
blood-root for sight
skunks for smell
crab apples for taste
yarrow for sound
mallow for touch.
Some we found named ill, too little or too much
or in a foreign tongue.
These we challenged with new names.

Space was our pre-occupation,
infinity, not eternity our concern.
We were strong bent on counting,
the railroad ties, so many to a mile,
the telephone poles, the cars that passed,
marking our growth against the door frames.

The sky was a kite,
I flew it on a string, winding
it in to see its blue, again
to count the whirling swallows,
and read the patterned scroll of
                         blackbirds turning

to check the markings of the hawk,
and then letting it out to the end
of the last pinched inch of
string, in the vise of thumb and finger.

Onc day the string broke,
the kite fled over the shoulder of the world,
but reluctantly, reaching back in great lunges
as lost kites do, or as a girl running
in a reversed movie, as at each
                              arched step, the earth
set free, leaps forward, catching
her farther back
the treadmill doubly betraying,
Remote and more remote.

Now I lie on a west facing hill in October
the dragging string having circled
                              the world, the universe,
crosses my hand in the grass. I do not grasp it,
it brushes my closed eyes, I do not open
That world is no longer mine,
                              but for remembrance
Space ended then, and time began.

Eugene McCarthy

37

THE YOUNG VIOLINIST

Childhood dreams of fame can come to a sudden
end; the experience is a natural part of growing up.
In this passage from Where Nothing Is Long Ago,
Virginia Sorenson tells of her childhood
hopes for stardom as a violinist:

Just before I was promoted to the sixth grade, my
teacher had paused one day at my desk. "I liked
your poem," she said in a low voice. "Maybe you'll
be a writer some day."

It was an unforgettable moment. After school I
stopped at the library and selected some books of
poems to take home. And in my journal I made
an excited entry with an illustration. The poem
the teacher spoke of had been printed, actually
printed, in the *Juvenile Instructor,* a magazine
published in Salt Lake City. Carol had sent it in
and so became responsible, as I tell her to this day,
for the infection of print which has never left me.

But in the diary I wrote: "I am going to be
either a writer or a violinist. I think I'll work on
both and leave the rest to The World and Fate."
I illustrated this sturdy sentiment with stick figures,
one with a fiddle, one at a desk with a feathered
pen, between them a large *"Which?"*

The World was never subjected to my fiddle,

for no child on earth ever brought so little so passionately to an instrument. For a year or so, Mother heroically insisted on daily practice, for she dreamed of a trio of sisters, Helen piano, I violin, Geraldine, 'cello. But nevertheless the poor woman firmly closed the kitchen door whenever I began to tune up. My violin she arranged to buy from a German convert who lived in the mouth of the canyon and ran the electric plant. His name was Brother Brox and his whole family was musical, he himself beguiling his lonely hours with lively tunes on his zither.

It was an illuminating session with my teacher, Miss Winifred Parry, one bright summer afternoon, that left writing indisputably in possession of my ambition. I had been learning positions and had come at last to the lesson on vibrato. All week I vibrated conscientiously, for was not vibrato the key to violinistic emotion? I played records on the Victrola, listening over and over to an Ave Maria with a shivering violin obbligato, accompanying it as best I could. I vibrated up and down the scales and went over every piece in my book, wondering at how they were altered and improved by my new technique. By Friday afternoon I was ready to show Miss Parry my immortal soul. She would, I fully expected, cry out, "Amazing! You should study abroad!" At the least I thought she might burst into happy teacher-tears.

To this day I can hear myself at the short warm-up scale, how I prepared for the revelation. With compressed lips and hot eyes, I began "Over the Waves."

Presently Miss Parry turned her back. I quavered on. I noticed that her shoulders were shaking. Proudly, I gave it all I had. And then, suddenly, she turned to me, her face scarlet with helpless laughter. She was one of those huge women with a round, pink face, very pretty, and shapely slender legs that never seemed to deserve the incongruous burden of weight above them. "Oh, *dear*—" she choked, and was off again.

So I knew.

A MEMORY FULL OF CHARM

In one of the most poetic passages of his Autobiography, *Mark Twain remembers the delightful times he spent on an uncle's farm:*

As I have said, I spent some part of every year at [my uncle's] farm until I was twelve or thirteen years old. The life which I led there with my cousins was full of charm, and so is the memory of it yet. I can call back the solemn twilight and mystery of the deep woods, the earthy smells, the faint odors

of the wild flowers, the sheen of rain-washed foliage, the rattling clatter of drops when the wind
shook the trees, the far-off hammering of wood-
peckers and the muffled drumming of wood pheas-
ants in the remoteness of the forest, the snapshot
glimpses of the disturbed wild creatures scurrying
through the grass—I can call it all back and make
it as real as it ever was, and as blessed.

I can call back the prairie, and its loneliness and
peace, and a vast hawk hanging motionless in
the sky, with his wings spread wide and the blue of
the vault showing through the fringe of their end
feathers. I can see the woods in their autumn dress,
the oaks purple, the hickories washed with gold,
the maples and the sumachs luminous with crim-
son fires, and I can hear the rustle made by the
fallen leaves as we plowed through them. I can see
the blue clusters of wild grapes hanging among
the foliage of the saplings, and I remember the
taste of them and the smell. I know how the wild
blackberries looked, and how they tasted, and the
same with the paw-paws, the hazelnuts, and the
persimmons; and I can feel the thumping rain,
upon my head, of hickory nuts and walnuts when
we were out in the frosty dawn to scramble for
them with the pigs, and the gusts of wind loosed
them and sent them down. I know the stain of
blackberries, and how pretty it is, and I know the

stain of walnut hulls, and how little it minds soap and water, also what grudged experience it had of either of them. I know the taste of maple sap, and when to gather it, and how to arrange the troughs and the delivery tubes, and how to boil down the juice, and how to hook the sugar after it is made, also how much better hooked sugar tastes than any that is honestly come by, let bigots say what they will. . . .

I can remember the bare wooden stairway in my uncle's house, and the turn to the left above the landing, and the rafters and the slanting roof over my bed, and the squares of moonlight on the floor, and the white cold world of snow outside, seen through the curtainless window. I can remember the howling of the wind and the quaking of the house on stormy nights, and how snug and cozy one felt, under the blankets, listening; and how the powdery snow used to sift in, around the sashes, and lie in little ridges on the floor and make the place look chilly in the morning and curb the wild desire to get up—in case there was any. I can remember how very dark that room was, in the dark of the moon, and how packed it was with ghostly stillness when one woke up by accident away in the night, and forgotten sins came flocking out of the secret chambers of the memory and wanted a hearing; and how ill chosen the time seemed for this kind of business; and how dismal was the hoo-hooing of the owl and the wailing of the wolf, sent mourning by on the night wind.

I remember the raging of the rain on that roof, summer nights, and how pleasant it was to lie and listen to it, and enjoy the white splendor of the lightning and the majestic booming and crashing of the thunder. It was a very satisfactory room, and there was a lightning rod which was reachable from the window, an adorable and skittish thing to climb up and down, summer nights, when there were duties on hand of a sort to make privacy desirable.

LITTLE ABE

The boy who grew up to be President Lincoln showed, even at an early age, some of the qualities that would later endear him to his countrymen. They are described here by Benjamin Thomas in his biography, Abraham Lincoln:

Abe had talent as a mimic, and often imitated the preachers and politicians he had heard. Sometimes he mounted a stump to orate, bringing belly-laughs from the other laborers and causing them to slight their work, thereby evoking a sharp rebuke or cuff from his father for such nonsense. The traditions of

43

the community affirm his kindliness, his sense of fair play, his helpfulness to others, his love of dumb animals, his ambition to excel. His neighbors remembered his laconic speech. They also remembered that plowing, hoeing, grubbing, and making fences held little attraction for him. The Lincoln farm was small, and Thomas often hired out the boy to work for neighbors. Abe did what was expected of him, but he showed no zeal about it, for he much preferred to read. One man recalled how he would take a book to the fields, so that at the end of each plow furrow he could read while allowing the horse to "breathe."

Abe was generally accounted lazy except for his desire to learn. But his progress in education was amazing for one who had such meager opportunities. He could spell down all the other pupils in school. He did all the writing for his family and much of it for their neighbors. At home he ciphered on boards when he had no paper or slate, shaving off the ciphering with a hunting-knife to start afresh. In a copybook in the smooth round script that became so easily distinguishable in his later years, he composed a bit of boyish doggerel, the earliest known specimen of his handwriting:

Abraham Lincoln, his hand and pen,
He will be good but God knows when.

44

ADLAI STEVENSON

During his years in public life, Adlai Stevenson had various occasions to recall his youth and the joys of childhood in general. Following are some of his comments:

My parents were vitamin conscious. How often my mother used to call me at play from the door, "Adlai, come and get your orange juice,"—a call that did not make me popular with new playmates!

I rarely take orange juice now.

There has been a lot of flattering talk on the theme of "home town boy makes good." It ought to be the other way around—good home town makes boy.

You know, in America any boy may become President, and I suppose it's just one of the risks he takes!

Spotting children in his campaign audiences, Adlai Stevenson was occasionally fond of asking, "How many children would like to be a candidate for President of the United States?" *Most of the children would raise their hands. Then Stevenson would ask,* "And how many candidates for the Presidency would like to be children again?" *At which point he would raise his own hand.*

THE MEANING OF
CHILDHOOD

A PARENT'S MISSION

In his autobiography, Everything But Money,
*humorist Sam Levenson expresses his philosophy
about the obligation we have to every child:*

I believe that each newborn child arrives on earth
with a message to deliver to mankind. Clenched in
his little fist is some particle of yet unrevealed truth,
some missing clue, which may solve the enigma of
man's destiny. He has a limited amount of time to
fulfill his mission and he will never get a second
chance—nor will we. He may be our last hope. He
must be treated as top sacred.

In a cosmos in which all things appear to have
a meaning, what is *his* meaning? We who are older
and presumably wiser must find the key to unlock
the secret he carries within himself. The lock cannot be forced. Our mission is to exercise the kind of
loving care which will prompt the child to open his
fist and offer up his truth, his individuality, the ir-
reducible atom of his self. We must provide the
kind of environment in which the child will joy-
fully deliver his message through complete self-ful-
fillment.

'LACED WITH MANY GOLDEN THREADS'

The happy memories of childhood are the ones which endure with the greatest vigor. So writes television commentator Eric Sevareid in this excerpt from This Is Eric Sevareid:

A child's heart is not made for desolation; it is made for warmth and love, and these it will always find, however hidden in the most barren places. These [last] thirty years my memories have been laced with many golden threads. I do not know if the psychologists are right, that we tend to remember the sweet and to forget the harsh, but for me in these thirty years the golden threads have outlasted the black.

They are composed of many things—shade and the cool grass of our yard, pleasant faces that never die, the creak of saddles and the smell of horses, the nectar of cactus berries and the stain of plums, the secret, devilish gang-thrill on Halloween, the cold dripping joy of the ice wagon in the hot summer street, the leafy path to the swimming hole, the mad joy of the circus parade down Main Street, the heady drug of printer's ink in the *Journal* shop, the girl of silver and blue, the stately gravity of the Chautauqua lecturer who made me feel so wise and grave on the walk home with Father.

What man does not remember and cherish such things? We are all alike, we graying American men who were boys in the small towns of our country. We have a kind of inverted snobbery of recollection and we are sometimes bores about it, but that's the way it is.

'A CHILD'S FAITH'

Robert Louis Stevenson, whose writings still delight children and adults alike, writes here about a child's capacity for imagination, and the unique and separate world it creates for him:

Nothing can stagger a child's faith; he accepts the clumsiest substitutes and can swallow the most staring incongruities. The chair he has just been besieging as a castle or valiantly cutting to the ground as a dragon is taken away for the accommodation of a morning visitor and he is nothing abashed, he can skirmish by the hour with a stationary coalscuttle; in the midst of the enchanted pleasance he can see without sensible shock the gardener soberly digging potatoes for the day's dinner.

He can make abstraction of whatever does not fit into his fable; and he puts his eyes into his pocket, just as we hold our noses in an unsavoury lane. And so it is, that although the ways of children cross with those of their elders in a hundred places daily, they never go in the same direction nor so much as lie in the same element.

So may the telegraph wires intersect the line of the highroad or so might a landscape painter and a bagman visit the same country, and yet move in different worlds.

'PIZZA PIES AND FIG BARS'

Children at the table can sometimes behave with less than perfect manners, as playwright Jean Kerr knows well. The following commentary is an excerpt from her book, The Snake Has All The Lines:

The first point to be established is that one does not sit *on* the table. One sits on the chair, and in such a way that all four legs touch the floor at the same time. (I am of course speaking of the four legs of the chair; children only *seem* to have four legs.) For children who will rock and tilt anyway, I suggest (a) built-in benches, (b) the practice of instilling in such children a sense of noblesse oblige, so that when they go crashing back onto their heads they go bravely and gallantly and without pulling the tablecloth, the dinner, and a full set of dishes with them. This last may sound severe, but it will be excellent training if they should ever enter the Marines, or even Schrafft's.

We don't have to bother about little niceties such as which fork is the shrimp fork (at these prices, who is giving them shrimp?). We will suppose, and safely, that the child has only one fork. If this child is interested in good manners and/or the sanity of his parents, he will not use the fork to (a) comb his hair, (b) punch holes in the tablecloth, or (c) remove buttons from his jacket. Nor will he ever, under any circumstances, place the tines of the fork under a full glass of milk and beat the handle with a spoon.

So far as the food itself is concerned, it would be well for the child to adopt a philosophical attitude about that dreary procession of well-balanced meals by reminding himself that in eighteen years or less he will be free to have frozen pizza pies and fig bars every single night. And he should remember, too, that there is a right way and a wrong way to talk about broccoli. Instead of the gloomy mutter, "Oh, broccoli again—ugh!" how much better the cheery "I guess I'll eat this broccoli first and get it over with."

Finally, children should be made to understand that no matter how repellent they find a given vegetable, they may not stuff large handfuls of it into their pockets, particularly if the vegetable is

creamed. This sorry but unfortunately common practice not only deprives the child of necessary vitamins but frequently exposes him to intemperate criticism and even physical violence.

'THE IDEALISM OF YOUTH'

Albert Schweitzer, in his Memoirs of Childhood and Youth, *offers these profound thoughts to grown-ups about the knowledge of life which they should pass on to their children:*

Grown-up people reconcile themselves too willingly to a supposed duty of preparing young ones for the time when they will regard as illusion what now is an inspiration to heart and mind. Deeper experience of life, however, advises their inexperience differently. It exhorts them to hold fast, their whole life through, to the thoughts which inspire them. It is through the idealism of youth that man catches sight of truth, and in that idealism he possesses a wealth which he must never exchange for anything else. . . .

As one who tries to remain youthful in his thinking and feeling, I have struggled against facts and experience on behalf of belief in the good and the true. At the present time when violence, clothed in life, dominates the world more cruelly than it ever has before, I still remain convinced that truth, love, peaceableness, meekness, and kindness are the violence which can master all other violence. The world will be theirs as soon as ever a sufficient number of men with purity of heart, with strength, and with perseverence think and live out the thoughts of love and truth, of meekness and peaceableness.

The knowledge of life, therefore, which we grown-ups have to pass on to the younger generation will not be expressed thus: "Reality will soon give way before your ideals," but "Grow into your ideals, so that life can never rob you of them." If all of us could become what we were at fourteen, what a different place the world would be!

'LOVE OF RITUAL'

In The World of Children, *the British authoress Elizabeth Taylor writes about children's love of ritual and repetition—a love which can seem almost endless until it is suddenly outgrown:*

One of the things we can be surest of with children is their love of ritual and repetition—the same old story that they know by heart, the same games played in the same way, the same pattern of Christmas and birthday. They love to know the way things are going, and pleasures repeated are intensified. There is none of that superstitious feeling that grown people have of "never going back."

One little boy we fetch from London to stay with us every holiday, gets into the car, and before we have driven out of his street, he leans over my husband's seat and says, "Go on, sing that song." Farther on, my husband must stop to buy me a bunch of flowers at a certain spot, because once he did. And as soon as he reaches our house, the child goes to a cupboard, and puts on an enormous pair of Wellington boots, in which he slops happily and familiarly about. He remembers his own beaker and his own place at the table, and he picks up family phrases again, as if they have never been off his lips. But I wait for the day when he will suddenly say, "Why do you always buy the flowers at *that* place?" or "Why must I always sit here with my back to the window?"

For many years, whenever my husband drove through a certain railway-tunnel the children clamoured for him to blow the horn, loving its echo. He came to do it automatically, and went on doing so too long. "Why on earth do you always do that?" he was one day asked.

TO DO AS YOU PLEASE

*In childrens' eyes, adults may look like giants
who live and act with complete freedom, doing
whatever they wish. Writer Leontine Young
describes this child's-eye-view in her book,*
Life Among The Giants:

Children want to be big for very practical reasons.
In the first place they are convinced that big people can do whatever they want. At least this is
the way it looks to newcomers of two and three
years. That is a state they ardently desire to attain
for themselves, and the whole matter looks relatively uncomplicated except for that persistent
snag, size. You could reach for that second piece of
cake with impunity if you were as big as the grown-
ups. Furthermore, careful observation indicates
that grownups are usually more respectful to other
grownups than to small people, and size appears to
be the answer. All of this adds up to power, and
power, as all children observe, is the key to a good
number of desirable states.

Power is the right to go to bed when you please,
eat as many helpings of cake as you like, grab whatever toys you want, command from big people
whatever services appeal to you, get rid of such an-
noying rivals as the new baby and ensure at all

times a devoted and attentive audience for whatever fleeting thoughts you might want to communi-
cate. It is all vaguely reminiscent of an ancient
Oriental potentate. Like the potentate, the young
are blankly unaware of any such moral abstractions
as justification and responsibility. Power means you
can do as you please, and from the vantage point
of two years that can seem an accurate observation
of the giants in any small one's life.

The giants are apt to have quite a different view-
point of the situation and may be relatively oblivi-
ous to the premises of the young. They are all too
conscious of the limitations of their power, the accompanying burdens of responsibility, the neces-
sities and the choices with their inevitable chain of
consequences. They have a past and a future as
well as a present, and the combination is likely to
be a considerable check on any impulsive, if soul-
satisfying, gestures. It's not easy in the midst of all
the complications to recognize that the small one
is right too. The giants do have total power. The
way they use it and the consequences of what they
do are different matters, and children with their
customary penchant for getting to the heart of a
situation start with the fact of power.

This is still fine as long as everyone is agreeing
and there's no occasion for any test of that power.
The trouble comes up when what a small citizen

wants and what his particular giant decides do not coincide. Then the dilemma becomes acute. There are only two possible answers for the young one. Give up the whole idea and go along with the giant's decision or find some way to outwit, seduce or outlast him until the situation conforms to his satisfaction. Either way can involve quite an expenditure of energy on the part of both parties.

'A CHILD'S WORLD'

In her book, The Sense of Wonder, *conservationist Rachel Carson tells of a child's clear and fresh vision of the world—a vision which must be carefully tended if it is not to be lost by adulthood:*

A child's world is fresh and new and beautiful, full of wonder and excitement. It is our misfortune that for most of us that clear-eyed vision, that true instinct for what is beautiful and awe-inspiring, is dimmed and even lost before we reach adulthood.

If I had influence with the good fairy who is supposed to preside over the christening of all children, I should ask that her gift to each child in the world be a sense of wonder so indestructible that it would last throughout life, as an unfailing antidote against the boredom and disenchantment of later years, the sterile preoccupation with things that are artificial, the alienation from the sources of our strength.

If a child is to keep alive his inborn sense of wonder without any such gift from the fairies, he needs the companionship of at least one adult who can share it, rediscovering with him the joy, excitement and mystery of the world we live in.

TO ENTER THE
KINGDOM OF HEAVEN

At that time the disciples came to Jesus, saying, "Who is the greatest in the kingdom of heaven?" And calling to him a child, he put him in the midst of them, and said, "Truly, I say to you, unless you turn and become like children, you will never enter the kingdom of heaven. Whoever humbles himself like this child, he is the greatest in the kingdom of heaven.

"Whoever receives one such child in my name receives me; but whoever causes one of these little ones who believe in me to sin, it would be better for him to have a great millstone fastened around his neck and to be drowned in the depth of the sea. . . .

"See that you do not despise one of these little ones; for I tell you that in heaven their angels always behold the face of my Father who is in heaven."

Matthew 18:1-10 (RSV)

Set in Baskerville, the fine transitional face named for the 18th century English printer John Baskerville of Birmingham. Printed on Hallmark Eggshell Book paper. Designed by Claudia Becker.